FOREWORD

*L*et me tell you the story behind this book. It all started fourteen years ago. I was in my mid-thirties and the minister of a congregation in a medium-size city in the Midwest. Ever since I was a teenager, all I ever wanted to be was a clergyman. I attended a denominational college and majored in—what else?—religion. I went directly to seminary and earned two advanced degrees. Along the way I got married, and we had a child. I expanded my ministerial skills and experienced various successes in my work in the parish. I was set.

Then something happened I never planned on. Out of an experience of professional burnout and personal unhappiness, I left the pastoral ministry. I left behind all I had been preparing for. I felt as if I was leaving behind myself. In time I also left behind my marriage, much of my support system, most of my security, and many of my dreams.

For a long time I felt quite lost. I found I didn't know how to handle this terribly difficult time. I read whatever I could find about going through life changes, and I made two discoveries: there wasn't much to read, and most of what I read wasn't very helpful. I decided that if I made it through my own life change intact, I would one day create something that might help others. Thus, this book.

What did I learn? The process took longer than I expected. It hurt as much as I feared. Sometimes the way was as dark as I've ever known. But I also learned this: you can go through a trying time of transition and grow from it. You can be happy again, sometimes happier than you thought possible. You can find meaning in these events, even deep meaning.

Because of what I and others have experienced, I want to assure you that there is hope to be found as you make your way through change. I pray you'll find it in the pages that follow.

Jim Miller

Fort Wayne, Indiana

Change is everywhere.

Anything that exists, changes.

Everything that comes into being, passes from being.

The universe itself is constantly shifting and moving.

What's true of galaxies is just as true of the earth.

Grasslands turn into deserts, and are one day brought back again.

Water overtakes what once was dry land,

    for days at a time, or for eons.

Then dry land appears again.

Mountains are born and later they die,

    and, on their way to death, they change shape and even location.

And all around are changes more easily seen, more closely experienced:

    winter giving way to spring, summer folding into fall;

        day chasing night, night pursuing day.

All is flux,
nothing is stationary.
HERACLITUS

We are changing,
we have got to change,
and we can no more help it
than leaves can help going yellow
and coming loose in autumn.
D. H. LAWRENCE

The old order changeth, yielding place to new,
And God fulfills Himself in many ways,
Lest one good custom should corrupt the world.
ALFRED, LORD TENNYSON

Change is also within us and within others.
Infants turn into toddlers,
  children grow into adolescents,
    and adults mature in ways no less striking, no less amazing.
New life continually presses to burst forth,
  even as older life presses to burst free.
Yet however much human change is predictable, it is equally unpredictable.
Jobs terminate with little notice.
Relationships come to an end for all sorts of reasons,
  and sometimes for no reason at all.
Illness strikes, accidents happen, tragedies occur,
  and bodies, minds, and spirits are changed for a time or forever.
People die, expectedly and unexpectedly,
  and life is suddenly altered for those who survive,
    never to be the same again.
There is no question: change is a constant in life.

All change is uncomfortable.
Even when it is desired, change can be disturbing,
for it disrupts your normal way of doing things.
It introduces the unknown, the unexperienced.
And when change comes your way against your wishes or will,
it can jar you even more.
It can leave you feeling disoriented.
It can call into question your strength and confidence.
Strong emotions may arise within you,
ones you'd rather not face, or ones you don't know *how* to face.
Whatever this change means to you,
at one time or another it will create a sense of unease.
Or it may bring something even more unpleasant—
a pain that won't go away.

Things do not change;
we change.
HENRY DAVID THOREAU

Change is not made without inconvenience,
even from worse to better.
RICHARD HOOKER

All changes, even the most longed for,
have their melancholy;
for what we leave behind is part of ourselves;
we must die to one life before we can enter another.
ANATOLE FRANCE

Contrary to what you may think, change need not be passively accepted.

You can participate in it and learn from it.

Sometimes you can direct it, while at other times it will direct you.

You always have a choice—

the choice of how you will respond.

You can approach change as a friend or as a foe,

as a catastrophe or as a challenge.

In other words, you can try to ward it off or you can welcome it.

This book will encourage you to welcome change.

You'll be introduced to wisdom

from those who have managed transitions.

You'll be offered suggestions for ways to approach your own transitions.

And you'll be led to look at three phases in the changes you experience:

a beginning, which is also an ending;

an ending, which is no less than a glorious beginning;

and, in between, a fertile period which may not seem that way at all.

We will begin at the natural starting place—the ending.

I

The beginning is an ending.

What we call the beginning is often an ending
And to make an end is to make a beginning.
The end is where we start from.

T. S. ELIOT

Every beginning is a consequence.
Every beginning ends something.
PAUL VALÉRY

Great is the art of beginning,
but greater the art of ending.
HENRY WADSWORTH LONGFELLOW

Keep constantly in mind in how many things
you yourself have already witnessed changes.
The universe is change, life is understanding.
MARCUS AURELIUS

The beginning of any transition is not really a beginning—it's an ending.
You realize you cannot have what you once had,

    or you can no longer do what you once did.

Something is gone from your life.

These endings appear in many forms.

Someone you love may have died,

    or an important relationship may have come to an end.

You may have lost some part of yourself—

    your physical health, your emotional well-being, your spiritual wholeness.

You may be leaving behind your job, or your home, or your family.

You may be called upon to say farewell to your innocence or security,

    your hopes or dreams, your past or future.

If this change is one you're looking forward to,

    you may not be expecting endings at all.

But they're there, just the same.

Endings do not arrive alone; they are accompanied by feelings.
Whether the loss is minor or major,
    whether the effect is fleeting or enduring,
        the result will be the same: a sense of grief.
Every person grieves differently, so your way will be like no one else's.
It would not be unusual, however, to experience shock or numbness at first,
    especially if your change is sudden or massive.
Sooner or later you may feel sad or depressed, anxious or afraid.
You may be slightly irritated or really infuriated.
Other feelings are also common: loneliness, fatigue, guilt, shame.
So are relief, gratitude, joy, love.
Your emotions may come and go quickly and unpredictably,
    or they may settle over you and refuse to leave.
You may find that you respond more strongly than you expect.
Or you may respond hardly at all.
Sometimes that happens, too.

The best way out is always through.
ROBERT FROST

*A*dversity reveals genius,
prosperity conceals it.
HORACE

*F*or every complex problem there is an easy answer,
and it is wrong.
H. L. MENCKEN

I learn by going where I have to go.
THEODORE ROETHKE

The best route to take is *through* your endings, not around them.

Your best approach is to express your feelings, not hide them or hide from them.

This may seem unusual or unwise, since it runs against popular ideas—

that a life of happiness has no room for sadness,

or that progress is always and only an upward movement,

or that gaining is without question better than losing.

When an ending comes into your life,

you have an opportunity to learn and show otherwise.

Whatever your emotions, you can honor them by expressing them.

By speaking them to a person or a group you trust,

you can gain both perspective and support.

By putting your feelings in writing, or music, or some other physical form,

you can channel a powerful energy so it's released constructively.

19

Your future will be influenced by the way you undergo this change,
   so you will do well to maximize your chances for success.
It's important to take care of yourself,
   for you need all the strength and stamina you can muster.
Be healthy in your eating and drinking.
Get the exercise you need and the rest you deserve.
Call upon others for help when you need them,
   and accept people's offers of assistance when they come.
Put off critical decision-making until you're sure the time is right.
In as many ways as you can, trust the process of change.
You may not understand all that's happening, or why it's happening,
   but try to believe that there is a principle at work here.
Operate under the belief that you are being led toward growth and healing,
   and day by day your way will become more clear.

*God, give me grace to accept with serenity
the things that cannot be changed,
the courage to change the things that should be changed,
and the wisdom to distinguish the one from the other.*
REINHOLD NIEBUHR

*Historic continuity with the past is not just a duty.
It is a necessity.*
OLIVER WENDELL HOLMES

*Real development is not leaving things behind, as on a road,
but drawing life from them, as from a root.*
G. K. CHESTERTON

In this time of discontinuity, it will help to remember your continuities.

No matter what has changed in your life, some things have not changed.

Now is the time to recall those things and treasure them.

Whatever inner strength you've known before, you can draw on it again.

However resilient you've been, however practical, however tenacious,

you can be that way again because you know how.

You have worked your way through other upheavals in life,

and you can apply now what you've learned from those times.

If someone you love is now gone from your life, others remain,

and while they cannot replace the one you're missing,

they can at least be with you during this time.

Above all else, you can turn to that Source of Hope

who is ready to hold you and lift you even when others cannot.

For there is a God who never changes, even when everything else seems to.

SUGGESTIONS

Journal.
Buy a notebook. Each day write about what's happening—what you're missing, feeling, hoping for. Don't worry about spelling and grammar. Just let what is inside you flow out as naturally as possible. This is meant just for your eyes. Date each entry. Weeks or months later, go back over what you've written. Pick out themes. Notice your growth. Highlight turning points. Congratulate yourself on your progress.

Build your self-esteem.
Times of change can rob you of confidence. There are things you can do to restore your self-esteem. Create small cards, each containing a validation: "I am growing," "I am worthy," and "I have every reason to hope," for starters. Add some that speak from your own life and some that remind you of what others have said. Put the cards where you'll see them throughout your day. Save greeting cards with affirming thoughts. Reread meaningful letters. Recall compliments people have given you. Pat yourself on the back every chance you get.

Talk with someone.
Talking with another is one of the healthiest things you can do. Find someone with whom you feel comfortable and ask them if they'll listen to your story. Share what you're going through and how it affects you. Speak with a person who's been through something similar. Is there a support group you might join? Check with your mental health center, the social work department of your local hospital, or your pastor, priest, or rabbi to learn what the options are. Might an appointment with a professional listener be a good solution? Remember that refusing to talk can slow your progress.

Practice relaxation techniques.
Take fifteen or twenty minutes twice a day to relax your whole body. Sit upright in a comfortable chair or lie down in a quiet place. Uncross your legs and arms. Close your eyes. Breathe slowly and deeply. Clear your mind more and more each time you exhale.

Beginning with your legs, tense the muscles for five seconds and then, while you take ten deep breaths, gradually let the tension out. Do this with your arms, abdomen, chest and shoulders, back, neck and jaw, forehead and scalp. Repeat this cycle several times. Once you feel relaxed, breathe rhythmically for another five minutes before stretching your body and opening your eyes. Another option is to try a relaxation audiotape. Read a book on deep relaxation and experiment until you find methods that work for you.

Mark your endings.
If you're experiencing the ending of a significant relationship or the loss of something crucial, you may find value in observing this change ritually. People sometimes light candles or frame pictures or create scrapbooks to honor their memories. A ring might be ceremonially removed or given away. A special site might be visited, a possession might be preserved or bequeathed, a flower or tree might be planted. You might want others to witness this time with you, or you may choose to do it alone.

Read something inspirational.
Allow yourself to be lifted by whatever you find inspiring. The Psalms can be especially meaningful during transition periods because of their enduring themes and honest human expression. If your time seems like an ordeal, try Psalm 6, 86, 102, or 123. For hope and assurance, turn to Psalm 23, 56, 62, and 139. Read something each day as you awaken and before you go to sleep.

Meditate and pray.
Make prayer part of your devotional reading. Find pockets of time for prayer through-out your day. If words do not flow, try this 400-year-old prayer by Lancelot Andrewes:

Lord, be thou within me, to strengthen me; without me, to keep me;
above me, to protect me; beneath me, to uphold me;
before me, to direct me; behind me, to keep me from straying;
round about me, to defend me.

II

In between is emptiness—fertile emptiness.

The night is the mother of the day
The winter of the spring
And even upon old decay
The greenest mosses cling.

JOHN GREENLEAF WHITTIER

—*So short a time*
To teach my life its transpositions to
This difficult and unaccustomed key!
EDNA ST. VINCENT MILLAY

Search the darkness, don't run from it.
Night travelers are full of light.
And you are, too; don't leave this companionship.
JELALUDDIN RUMI

You grew weary from your many wanderings,
but you did not say, "It is useless."
You found your desire rekindled,
and so you did not weaken.
ISAIAH 57:10

You need the patience of the husbandman, who,
after committing the seed to the earth,
does not disturb the soil every day
to see whether it is growing.
PHILALETHES

A middle period separates the beginning of a transition from its end.

Most likely, you won't know when it starts.

Phases of change dissolve from one into another almost without notice.

They may even overlap for a while.

Yet eventually you'll come to realize you're in a "between" time.

If the change you're going through is painful and traumatic,

this period may seem long, arduous, and depressing.

It's like an interminable winter when the cold refuses to leave,

the sun refuses to shine, and the earth is delayed in its thaw.

The world around you seems lifeless and dreary,

and so does your world within.

Your feelings may still overwhelm you at times,

but it's just as likely they'll become dulled and muted.

Even if the change is one you've looked forward to,

you'll probably experience "in-between" feelings nonetheless,

for you must let go of what has been

before you can grasp what will be.

This middle period will take as long as it takes.

Its duration cannot be foretold.

Two processes are at work here.

One is the external change—

  you might go from being single to being married,

    from being married to being widowed,

      from being employed to being unemployed,

      from being healthy to being ill.

The other process, your internal transition, is altogether different.

Whatever the speed of the changes around you,

  you must undergo your own rate of adjustment

    to those changes that take place within you.

This period cannot be rushed, much as you might want it to be.

Deep within, you are shifting ever so slowly.

Renewal is taking shape ever so gradually.

If you push ahead too quickly, you'll restrict what's forming carefully, fragilely.

*Not until we are lost
do we begin to understand ourselves.*
HENRY DAVID THOREAU

*One must not always think so much
about what one should do,
but rather what one should be.*
MEISTER ECKHART

*Where thou hesitatest between two courses of action,
choose always the one which leaves thee more alone,
more in silence, more in love.*
SISTER CONSOLATA

*The question is not: why did it happen this way,
or where is it going to lead you,
or what is the price you will have to pay.
It is simply: how are you making use of it?
And about that there is only one who can judge.*
DAG HAMMARSKJÖLD

There is an emptiness to this part of your transition—
a hollowness that is exactly what you need.
Looking back, you will realize the key word
for your beginning time was *feeling*—
your main task was to free yourself to feel whatever welled up within.
The key word for this middle time is *being*—just being.
Be in the emptiness, and let it become a temporary home,
where you can make real the truth that the past is past.
Be in the quietness and allow its serenity to soothe you.
Be in the barrenness and let its austere beauty teach you and comfort you.
Be in the openness and attend to what is happening inside you—
a desire to be idle or alone, to meditate or meander,
to connect or re-connect.
Be in the moment and savor what it holds.
It may be less than before,
but it can be enough for now.

You are being given a natural time-out.
Poised between the past and the future,
  you're in position to assess where you've come from
      and where you're headed.
What has brought you to this place in life?
Are you satisfied with choices you've made?
Do you wish to rethink any decisions?
Now is an ideal time to re-examine your priorities.
In light of your recent experiences,
  what has become really important to you?
If you were told your time on earth was suddenly limited,
  what changes would you hurry to make?
What prevents you from beginning those changes now?

I wait for the Lord, my soul waits,
and in his word I hope;
my soul waits for the Lord
more than those who watch for the morning.

PSALM 130:5–6A

Change is the nursery
Of music, joy, life, and eternity.

JOHN DONNE

What an extraordinary situation is that of us mortals!
Each of us is here for a brief sojourn;
for what purpose he knows not,
though he sometimes thinks he feels it.

ALBERT EINSTEIN

God is neither here nor there:
whosoever desires to find Him,
let him chain his hands and feet, body and soul.

ANGELUS SILESIUS

Another opportunity awaits you in this "between" time,
and that is the opportunity to give voice to your soul.
This can be a wonderful time to deepen your spiritual life,
for this period shares many characteristics
associated with religious retreats and pilgrimages.
You are necessarily more alone, even if others are around,
for this is *your* transition—no one else can experience it for you.
You are a step removed from everyday routine, and perhaps far removed.
You face questions for which you do not yet have answers,
and for which your old answers may no longer work.
You are on a search for something bigger than you, something deeper.
And in your heart you know it's not something, but Something.
Or Someone.
When that awareness comes, your transition becomes a time of the Eternal.
If you're fortunate,
you will know the experience of searching until you are found.

SUGGESTIONS

Visit prior transitions.

Go back over significant changes you've made through the years. List them on paper so you can see them easily. Learn what you can from this list. Have you experienced few or many transitions? How many have been chosen by you and how many dictated for you? How serious or traumatic have they been? How have you responded in each case? What do you remember about the "between" times of those transitions? How long did they last? What helped you through them? What does this say about the time you're in now?

Take respites.

Even if this is a heavy time for you, you don't have to be weighed down constantly or completely. Give yourself breaks from the pressures and responsibilities. Go to a movie or play, a ball park or museum. Spend time with people you like. Read something light-hearted. Listen to something entertaining. Say something amusing. Do something frivolous. When you return from these experiences, you'll not just feel fresher—you'll be fresher.

Rub up against nature.

Take long walks outside. Breathe the air deeply. Study the clouds. Inspect the trees. Nuzzle the flowers. If you can, lie back to back with the earth. Gather the lessons in each sunset and sunrise, in each fall and spring, in winter storms and summer rain. Ponder seeds and sprouts, leaves and limbs, the tiny and the tremendous. You'll learn, not just about the beauty of changes in creation, but about the beauty of the changeless Creator.

Inventory your resources.

Be clear about what you have going for you. Get it down in black and white. List the strengths you've developed that can help you through this time: the skills you've acquired through the years, the advantages that are yours. Name individuals to whom you can turn for specific needs: emotional support, cognitive guidance, tangible assistance, surefire fun. Include your informal networks as well as formal organizations. Keep this list nearby. You can never tell when it will come in handy.

Visualize ideal outcomes.
The only way to get where you want to go is to know where that place is. What do you want your future to look like? In the best of all possible worlds, given what has happened to you, how would you like your days and nights to be spent? Where will you live? How will you work? Who will be included in your life? What will add meaning to your days? What will you add to other people's lives? Start by visualizing your ideal and work your way to the real.

Make a retreat.
Get away somewhere and concentrate on your spiritual life, especially as it relates to this transition of yours. Is there a monastery or retreat center nearby? Might there be a spiritual director with whom you can speak? Another option is to attend a conference or weekend workshop built around a spiritual theme. Watch newspapers and magazines for upcoming events. Check with your pastor, the local clergy association, people in other congregations, or the chaplaincy department of your hospital. If you're hesitant to try a retreat by yourself, ask a friend to go with you.

Pray in a new way.
In his first letter to the Thessalonian Christians, Saint Paul gives this advice: "Pray constantly." This is good, simple advice for you as well. Whatever you're doing, do it as a prayer. Be consciously grateful for what you can see and hear and do. Offer short, nonverbal prayers when you meet someone or remember them, for those you know and those you don't know. Throughout the day, pray for yourself in an honest, accepting, forgiving way. Pray for things you never think to pray for. Pray for your transitions.

III

At the end is a new beginning.

And nd yes I said yes I will Yes!

JAMES JOYCE

Awake, my heart, and sing!
PAUL GERHARDT

*The real voyage of discovery consists
not in seeking new landscapes
but in having new eyes.*

MARCEL PROUST

The only joy in the world is to begin.
CESARE PAVESE

*There is nothing more difficult to take in hand,
more perilous to conduct, or more uncertain in its success,
than to take the lead in the introduction of a new order of things.*
INSCRIPTION ON MACHIAVELLI'S TOMB

*Patient endurance
Attains all things.*
TERESA OF AVILA

Internal beginnings have a way of creeping up on you.

One moment they're not there, the next they are.

Sometimes they come with a quiet rustle or soft whisper.

Other times they announce themselves with fanfare.

However they make themselves known, beginnings carry with them
an energy that is unmistakable and a promise that is undeniable.

For, as much as anything, beginnings are life's way of saying, "Yes!"

Yes, whatever has happened, something new can happen.

Yes, whatever has disappeared, something original can appear,
or something significant can reappear.

And, yes, this can occur not just around you, but within you.

Your beginnings are no more important than your endings,
no more worthwhile than your interim periods.

They're simply that next step in your growth,
another chance to become more completely who you're meant to be.

You'll find a noticeable shift in this last period of your transition.

While the first phase emphasized *feeling*,

    and the second, *being*,

        the emphasis now is on *doing*.

You'll recognize this time when it appears:

    you'll feel drawn toward doing what comes next, what comes naturally.

Something in touch with your past will want to reach toward your future.

The clearing away will have gone on long enough.

Now will come a time to add, to build, to move ahead.

Beginnings are enticing.

They beckon you to follow your longings.

And these are not old longings—

    those will have changed as a result of all you've been through.

Beginnings invite you to give substance to heartfelt dreams—

    dreams from former days that have taken on new shape,

        and dreams you've never spun before, but cannot resist spinning now.

As the hand is made for holding
and the eye for seeing,
Thou hast fashioned me for joy.
Share with me the vision that shall find it everywhere.

GAELIC PRAYER

When old words die out on the tongue,
new melodies break forth from the heart;
and where the old tracks are lost,
new country is revealed with its wonders.

RABINDRANATH TAGORE

Laugh and grow strong.

IGNATIUS LOYOLA

Weeping may linger for the night,
but joy comes with the morning.

PSALM 30:5

Real beginnings capture your imagination—they're fun.

They can evoke the child in you, whatever your age.

They may bring out the artist—that part of you that wants to create.

They may arouse the poet or the minstrel within you,

the clown or the lover, the mystic or the sage.

Your sense of joy will reawaken.

So will your sense of hope and your feelings of wonder.

Yet there's more to your beginnings than fun.

They often take work.

You may have to immerse yourself in details

and follow step-by-step procedures.

You may have to do what you thought you didn't want to do,

or didn't know how to do, or feared to do.

And yet you are compelled to move forward, to plunge ahead.

As your spirit returns and your energy resurfaces,
you may be inclined to rush ahead.
Wisdom offers this counsel: not too fast.
This is a time to pace yourself,
learning and savoring everything along the way.
It's a time to proceed gently.
Beginnings do not always go easily.
Trials may lead to errors—that's to be expected.
Exertion may cause fatigue—that's only natural.
This is a time also to be sensitive to others,
those undergoing their own changes and those adjusting to yours.
Ultimately, it is a time to accept responsibility for yourself:
for the part you've played in making you who you are,
and for the part you're now playing in who you're becoming.

Be still, and know that I am God.
PSALM 46:10A

Ask, and it will be given you;
search, and you will find;
knock, and the door will be opened for you.
JESUS OF NAZARETH

I want to be thoroughly used up when I die,
for the harder I work the more I live.
I rejoice in life for its own sake.
It is a sort of splendid torch
which I have got hold of for the moment,
and I want to make it burn as brightly as possible
before handing it on to future generations.
GEORGE BERNARD SHAW

This final phase will give you a viewpoint you haven't had before.

It's difficult to make sense of what is happening to you right when it happens.

But over the course of time, and through the eyes of experience,

   you will begin to piece together the significance.

You'll be able to see patterns of this transition and how they developed,

   problems that were solved and answers that were found.

You can start to understand how this happened and not that,

   or why this occurred among all the other possibilities,

      and what all this means for your life and other people's lives.

With this new perspective comes a vital opportunity—to search for meaning.

You can look beneath the obvious and find what really makes sense.

You can honor the mystery of events and admit you cannot know everything.

And you can abide with the unknown,

   confident that the Unknowable already abides with you,

      and always will.

SUGGESTIONS

Encourage creativity.

The last phase of your transition is easily the most creative. Brainstorm all the options you can think of, even the dumb ones. Ask the most imaginative persons you know to feed you their notions. Do your dreaming in a place new to you, a place you enjoy. Walk on a beach or traipse in the mountains. Sit in an open field. Make simple changes in how you do things. Draw with those great big crayons. Use your opposite hand. Spend an afternoon with a small friend's building blocks. Smile a lot. Expect something new to come to you and it will.

Ask for feedback.

If your transition has been long in unfolding, you'll find it helpful to get another perspective. Ask someone who knows you well to describe how they see you now, compared to the way you used to be. Which changes are most obvious? What are the little differences? What has impressed them about how you've handled this time? What input do they have about this new path you're on? Remember: not everyone will understand your changes. And don't forget this rule from the medical world: it's okay to get second and third opinions.

Write a dialogue.

Once you're well into your new beginning, compose a conversation between "Old Me" and "New Me." Have them talk to one another about what has happened. What does each want the other to know? Just scribble the first things that come to mind. Write until the dialogue has ended. Then read aloud what these two have said. What is there to affirm about Old Me? About New Me? Save what you've written and read it again in six months.

Name the lessons.

You cannot help but learn some worthwhile lessons in any transition. But what are they? Unless you name them, you do not really know them. Unless you can state them, they are not really yours. Write them clearly and simply, using no more than a sentence on each. Meditate on them. Carry them with you—in your mind and heart.

Tell your story.

Stories are powerful. They're also popular—everyone likes a good yarn. So go ahead: tell yours. If you've kept a journal, read back through it and then weave the tale as only you can do. Tell it in words or tunes, with paint or film, or whatever best suits you and your message. Compile a scrapbook. Edit a video. Do this for yourself if for no one else. You may be surprised how many people will find meaning in learning your story.

Share yourself.

You're in a unique position to help others who are in the midst of a transition. Because you've survived and grown from your experience, you can be more than just a help—you can be an inspiration. Offer what your experience tells you they might need. Perhaps you have practical information that will assist. Perhaps you can give them your listening ear, your knowing assurance. Perhaps you can offer them hope, simply by letting them see what you've accomplished, or what's been accomplished in you. Share the most valuable resource you have: yourself.

Learn from the stories of others.

Look into the lives of others who have undergone serious transitions, both the famous and the not-so-famous. How did they survive? What helped them? What hindered them? Where did they get their strength and inspiration? What happened to them as a result of the change? Delve into the biblical story of the Israelites as told in 2 Kings 25, when a huge change was forced upon them. Then read about how they responded, as preserved in Psalm 137.

Take something with you.

As you move on to other parts of your life, take this experience with you. Find or create a symbol that reminds you of what has happened and what you do not want to forget. Maybe this reminder is something you can frame and display where you live or work. Maybe you can place your symbol on a mantel or table or dashboard. Perhaps you can keep it near you on a necklace or key chain, or simply carry it in your pocket. Experiences of transition are too important to be left behind. Weave yours into your future.

CONCLUSION

Change will not change, but we can.

There is nothing in this world constant,
but inconstancy.
JONATHAN SWIFT

It is in change that things find rest.
HERACLITUS

*Few during their lifetime come anywhere near
exhausting the resources dwelling within them.
There are deep wells of strength that are never used.*
RICHARD E. BYRD

Arriving at one goal is the starting point of another.
JOHN DEWEY

*I find the great thing in this world
is not so much where we stand,
as in what direction we are moving.*
OLIVER WENDELL HOLMES

*Lord, we know what we are
but not what we may be.*
WILLIAM SHAKESPEARE

Change is here to stay.
It will always accompany you,
    because you are the way you are,
        and because life is the way it is.
There will continually be losses and endings in your life.
New things will be handed to you or grasped by you.
New beginnings will be made for you or by you.
Whatever the reasons for these shifts in your life,
    you cannot avoid them.
You cannot stop change.
But that does not mean that you are helpless in the face of change,
    or that you have no choices in the matter.
For you have one noteworthy freedom that cannot be taken from you.

If fate throws a knife at you,
there are two ways of catching it—
by the blade and by the handle.

ORIENTAL PROVERB

Everything can be taken away from a person but one thing:
the last of human freedoms—
to choose one's attitude in any given set of circumstances,
to choose one's own way.

VICTOR FRANKL

The choice is always ours.

ALDOUS HUXLEY

You are free to choose how you will respond to change in your life.

You may elect to see it as always and only a threat.

Or you may decide to explore the possibilities that come with it,

    however small or uncertain they may seem at the moment.

You may choose to read each change as a potential danger.

Or you may seek in it a note of invitation, of promise.

You may treat your transitions as problems that must be borne.

Or you may approach them as challenges that can broaden and enrich you.

The way you choose to see the changes around you and within you

    will determine how they affect your life,

      as well as how your life will affect them.

This is a decision only you can make.

It is a decision that is not without risks.

Fortunately, those risks can lead to life.

Lord of the world, show me one thing:
Show me what this, which is happening
at this very moment, means to me.
LEVI YITZHAK OF BERDICHEV

If I take the wings of the morning
and settle at the farthest limits of the sea,
even there your hand shall lead me,
and your right hand shall hold me fast.
PSALM 139:9-10

You, from whom to be turned is to fall,
to whom to be turned is to rise,
and in whom to stand is to abide forever:
Grant us in all our duties your help,
in all our perplexities your guidance,
in all our dangers your protection,
and in all our sorrows your peace.
AUGUSTINE OF HIPPO

Whether change chooses you or you choose change,
  it can still bring you new life.
You can discover strengths you never knew you possessed.
You can learn to be more flexible and resilient,
  more self-aware and self-assured.
You can increase your compassion as well as your concern for others,
  your love as well as your knowledge.
You can use this time to evaluate your priorities and values,
  to become clear about what's truly important for your time on earth.
You can gather significant life lessons you'll always carry with you.
In other words, you can do what a time of change so naturally encourages:
  make a fresh beginning.